I0427165

THE ART OF MINDFUL LEADERSHIP

Learn to Lead with Empathy, Translate Passion into
Purpose, Make Leadership Simple and Create a
Billion-Dollar Business.

PRADIP DAS

legal, financial, medical or professional advice. The content within this book has been derived from various sources. Please consult a licensed professional before attempting any techniques outlined in this book.

By reading this document, the reader agrees that under no circumstances is the author responsible for any losses, direct or indirect, which are incurred as a result of the use of information contained within this document, including, but not limited to, — errors, omissions, or inaccuracies.

Author Profile

Table of Contents

Introduction

Steve Jobs known for his revolutionary ideas, was not only an innovator but also a mindful leader. He believed in the power of focused attention and non-judgmental awareness— the essence of mindfulness.

Jobs often conducted walking meetings, engaging with his team while strolling through Apple's iconic campus. In these moments, he accepted the present, developing creativity and collaboration. His decisions, grounded in mindfulness, led to the creation of ground breaking products that changed the landscape of technology.

In another corner of the corporate world, Sundar Pichai, the CEO of Alphabet Inc., was weaving a narrative of empathetic leadership. Pichai understood that mindful leadership begins with self-awareness. He actively listened to his team, acknowledged their concerns, and promoted open communication. His mindfulness journey created a culture of empathy, where employees felt valued and supported.

On a different path, Arianna Huffington, the founder of Thrive Global, gave preference to mindful leadership. Having experienced burnout, Huffington recognized the importance of stress reduction and resilience. She championed well-being in the workplace, encouraging individuals to unplug, recharge, and prioritize mental health. Her commitment to mindfulness reflected a resilience that transformed not only her life but also the lives of those around her.

These stories create a fabric of mindful leadership—a journey of self-discovery, intentional decision-making, and compassionate collaboration. Mindful leaders like Jobs, Pichai, and Huffington understood that mindfulness is not a destination but a way of being. It is about embracing the present moment, acknowledging emotions, and building a positive work environment.

As leaders follow their mindful leadership journey, they find the power to transform challenges into opportunities. The story of mindful leadership is an invitation to leaders everywhere—a call to begin on a journey where authenticity, empathy, and resilience guide the way. Through mindfulness, leaders can create not only successful organizations but also workplaces that thrive on the principles of compassion, innovation, and lasting inner harmony.

Importance of Mindful Leadership

In the fast-paced, the importance of mindful leadership cannot be overstated. As the business world undergoes constant transformations, leaders equipped with mindfulness find themselves better positioned to navigate challenges, develop innovation, and cultivate a positive workplace culture.

At the heart of mindful leadership lies the ability to be fully present in the moment. In an era where distractions abound, leaders who practice mindfulness bring a heightened level of focus to their decision-making processes. This focused attention allows for a deeper understanding of complex situations, enabling leaders to make informed and strategic choices.

Mindful leaders also play a pivotal role in shaping the organizational culture. In a world where diversity, equity, and inclusion are paramount, mindfulness develops an environment of openness and acceptance. Leaders who practice mindfulness adopt diversity as a strength, recognizing and appreciating the unique perspectives each team member brings to the table.

In the pursuit of innovation, mindful leadership acts as a catalyst. By encouraging a culture that values creativity and out-of-the-box thinking, mindful leaders inspire their teams to approach challenges with fresh perspectives. The practice of mindfulness allows leaders to tap into their own creative reservoirs and, in turn, encourages a culture where innovative ideas flourish.

One of the significant challenges in modern organizations is the prevalence of stress and burnout. Mindful leadership addresses this issue head-on by promoting employee well-being. Leaders who prioritize mindfulness understand the importance of work-life balance and mental health. By creating spaces for mindfulness practices, such as meditation or wellness programs, organizations develop a healthier, more engaged workforce.

Furthermore, mindful leadership serves as a cornerstone for effective communication. In a world dominated by digital communication, misunderstandings can arise easily. Mindful leaders practice active listening and clear communication, reducing the likelihood of misinterpretations and developing stronger connections among team members.

As organizations navigate the complexities of the modern business landscape, mindful leadership emerges as a transformative force. It is not merely a leadership style but a way of being—a commitment to self-awareness, empathy, and continuous growth. By embracing mindful leadership, organizations can cultivate resilience, adaptability, and a harmonious workplace where both leaders and team members thrive in the face of change.

Mindfulness Practices

Mindful leadership is anchored in the practice of mindfulness. Mindfulness, rooted in ancient traditions, has found its place in modern leadership as a powerful tool for self-awareness, stress reduction, and improved decision-making.

Mindful Breathing: One of the simplest yet most effective mindfulness practices is mindful breathing. By directing attention to the breath, individuals can anchor themselves in the present moment. Leaders often use mindful breathing as a quick and accessible technique to regain focus during hectic schedules.

Body Scan Meditation: This practice involves a systematic, focused awareness of different parts of the body. By scanning the body with attention, individuals develop an acute awareness of bodily sensations, promoting relaxation and mindfulness. Leaders find the body scan meditation helpful for stress reduction and grounding themselves in high-pressure situations.

Mindful Walking: Incorporating mindfulness into daily activities, such as walking, can be transformative. Mindful walking involves paying attention to each step, the sensations in the feet, and the surrounding environment. Leaders often engage in mindful walking to recharge, developing a sense of clarity and connection with the present moment.

Loving-Kindness Meditation: Loving-kindness meditation involves cultivating feelings of love and compassion. Leaders who practice loving-kindness meditation develop a mindset of empathy and understanding. This practice extends beyond personal well-being to nurturing positive relationships within the workplace.

Mindful Listening: Effective communication is a cornerstone of mindful leadership, and mindful listening is a key component. Leaders consciously practice being fully present during conversations, giving their undivided attention to the speaker. This develops a deeper understanding of others and strengthens interpersonal connections.

Mindful Eating: In the hustle of leadership responsibilities, mealtimes can become rushed and mindless. Mindful eating encourages leaders to savor each bite, paying attention to the flavors, textures, and sensations. This practice not only promotes healthier eating habits but also serves as a moment of reflection and rejuvenation.

By incorporating these mindfulness practices into their routine, leaders lay the groundwork for a mindful leadership approach. These practices not only enhance personal well-being but also contribute to the creation of a mindful organizational culture, where individuals thrive and collaborate in an atmosphere of presence and awareness.

Mindfulness and Effective Leadership

In the journey of leadership, a powerful ally often overlooked is mindfulness. But what exactly is mindfulness, and how does it weave its magic in the realm of effective leadership? Let's explore this connection in simple terms, drawing inspiration from the life and principles of Mahatma Gandhi.

Understanding Mindfulness: At its core, mindfulness is about being fully present in the current moment, acknowledging and accepting one's thoughts and feelings without judgment. It's a mental state that develops clarity, focus, and a deep understanding of oneself and others. Now, let's see how this aligns with effective leadership.

Take Mahatma Gandhi, for instance. His leadership style was rooted in mindfulness. Amidst the chaos of India's fight for independence, Gandhi remained fully present, centered in his beliefs, and committed to nonviolent resistance. He acknowledged the challenges, felt the pulse of the nation, and understood the complex emotions of the people.

In the business world, mindful leaders exhibit a similar presence. They navigate challenges with a calm demeanor, acknowledging the realities without succumbing to panic. By understanding the thoughts and feelings of their team members, they build a more compassionate and empathetic leadership approach.

Mindful leaders, inspired by the Gandhi-like principles, make decisions with a clear mind, free from impulsive reactions. They create a work environment where employees feel valued, listened to, and understood. This develops a culture of trust and collaboration, essential ingredients for organizational success.

So, embracing mindfulness in leadership isn't just about personal well-being; it's a powerful tool to build stronger connections, make informed decisions, and lead with compassion. As you begin your journey toward mindful leadership, remember the profound impact it can have on your team, just as Gandhi's mindful approach left an indelible mark on the history of India's independence.

Clarity in Vision: Imagine a leader who sees the way forward with absolute clarity, like a bright path lit by unwavering principles. Mahatma Gandhi was such a leader—a symbol of mindful leadership. His vision for India's independence through nonviolent resistance was like a map, drawn from a deep understanding of the present reality and a strong commitment to make things better.

Gandhi's clarity of purpose and his unwavering principles were like a guiding light for his followers. His belief in nonviolence and his commitment to India's freedom were rooted in a profound understanding of the world around him.

Instead of reacting impulsively to challenges, he carefully considered the best way forward.

In today's complex world, where leaders often face numerous uncertainties, Gandhi's approach serves as an inspiration. His mindful leadership teaches us the importance of having a clear vision, understanding the current situation deeply, and committing to positive change. Gandhi's legacy reminds us that leadership guided by unwavering principles can lead to transformative and lasting impact.

Focused Decision-Making: Mindfulness is like a superpower that helps you stay fully concentrated on what you're doing. Think about Mahatma Gandhi, a real-life superhero of mindful decision-making. Every choice he made, from leading the famous Salt March to promoting peace between communities, was driven by a deep understanding of the possible outcomes and a dedication to the well-being of all. His decisions were like a carefully crafted dance with the present moment, showing us the incredible impact of being fully aware and focused. Just like Gandhi, we can use mindfulness to make decisions that truly matter, decisions that are rooted in the now and have a positive ripple effect on the world around us. It's not about looking back or worrying about the future; it's about being fully present, just like Gandhi was, and making choices that lead to a better tomorrow.

Emotional Intelligence: Mindful leaders stand out in emotional intelligence, skillfully comprehending and handling their own emotions while empathizing with others. Mahatma Gandhi exemplified these qualities. His leadership was characterized by profound compassion and empathy, enabling a powerful connection with the masses on an emotional level. This emotional resonance became a driving force behind the strength of the independence movement he spearheaded.

Gandhi's capacity to understand the emotions of the people he led, coupled with his genuine concern for their well-being, created a bond that went beyond mere leadership. He could sense the pulse of the nation, addressing not just its physical needs but also its emotional aspirations. By embodying emotional intelligence, Gandhi became not only a political leader but also a symbol of hope and unity, rallying people together through shared sentiments and a collective vision for a free and compassionate India. In the realm of mindful leadership, Gandhi's legacy continues to illuminate the path for leaders seeking to make a profound impact on both the emotional and tangible aspects of their followers' lives.

Resilience in Adversity: Leadership frequently encounters storms of challenges. Mindfulness serves as a foundation for resilience, which is the ability to gracefully navigate through adversity. Mahatma Gandhi's life exemplified remarkable resilience in the face of opposition, imprisonment, and personal sacrifices. His unwavering commitment to his principles and the cause he believed in demonstrated how mindfulness can empower leaders to endure and overcome challenges.

In simpler terms, think of resilience like a superhero power for leaders. It's what helps them stay strong and keep going, even when things get really tough. Gandhi, who was a great leader, showed us how powerful this superhero power can be. When he faced difficult times, like when people disagreed with him or when he was put in jail, he didn't give up. Instead, he stayed true to what he believed in, showing incredible strength and determination. This is what mindfulness does – it helps leaders bounce back from tough situations and keep going on their journey.

Effective Communication: Mindful leaders excel in communication, being fully engaged in conversations and attuned to others. Mahatma Gandhi, an iconic example, adopted truthful and straightforward communication. Whether through speeches, writings, or personal interactions, his expressions mirrored a profound awareness of the audience and a dedication to transparent, authentic communication. Gandhi's words were a beacon of simplicity, resonating with people from various walks of life. This mindful approach to communication not only developed understanding but also built trust and unity among those he led. As we reflect on Gandhi's legacy, his communication style serves as a timeless reminder of the impact authenticity and mindful engagement can have in creating connections and inspiring positive change.

Cultivating Empathy: A mindful leader possesses a unique ability to comprehend and acknowledge the thoughts and emotions of others. Mahatma Gandhi exemplified this quality through his deep empathy for the oppressed and marginalized. His unwavering commitment to social justice was fueled by a profound understanding of the challenges faced by those on the fringes of society. Gandhi's leadership, characterized by compassion and empathy, was a testament to his capacity to see the world through the eyes of others. This perspective allowed him to connect with people on a profound level, developing a sense of understanding and unity in the pursuit of a more just and equitable society.

In essence, mindfulness and effective leadership are intertwined. By embracing mindfulness, leaders can hone the qualities that define their effectiveness – clarity, focus, emotional intelligence, resilience, effective communication, and empathy. Mahatma Gandhi's life serves as a testament to the transformative power of mindful leadership, reminding us that a present and mindful approach can pave the way for effective and impactful leadership.

Leadership Challenges

In the ever-evolving landscape of the modern world, leadership faces a multitude of challenges, primarily driven by the fast-paced nature of the business environment.

Challenges posed by rapid technological advancements:

Technological innovations, though empowering, present a double-edged sword for leaders. The rapid pace of technological advancements demands continuous adaptation, often leaving leaders grappling with the dilemma of staying relevant. From artificial intelligence to blockchain, leaders must navigate through the complexities of these technologies while ensuring their teams are equipped with the necessary skills.

Consider a scenario where a leader in a traditional manufacturing industry suddenly faces the integration of automation and smart technologies. Adapting to these changes becomes a monumental challenge, requiring not only a strategic vision but also the ability to guide teams through the inevitable uncertainties.

The impact of globalization on leadership dynamics: Globalization has transformed the business landscape into an interconnected web of opportunities and challenges. While it opens doors to broader markets, it also intensifies competition and introduces diverse cultural dynamics.

Imagine a leader managing a team spread across different continents, each with its unique cultural nuances. Navigating through these differences, understanding local markets, and harmonizing a global strategy demand a level of leadership agility that goes beyond traditional approaches.

Leaders must grapple with the task of creating a cohesive organizational culture that respects diversity and develops collaboration across borders. The challenge lies not only in managing a geographically dispersed team but also in crafting a unified vision that resonates across diverse cultural contexts.

To address these challenges, leaders must adopt strategies that align with the dynamic nature of the modern business environment.

Agile Leadership: Embracing agile leadership principles allows leaders to respond swiftly to changes and uncertainties. An agile leader values flexibility, collaboration, and continuous learning, enabling them to steer the ship through the turbulent waters of technological disruptions and global shifts.

Investing in Continuous Learning: Recognizing the importance of continuous learning is paramount. Leaders need to cultivate a learning culture within their organizations, ensuring that teams are equipped with the skills required to navigate technological advancements and accept the opportunities presented by globalization.

Cultivating Emotional Intelligence: As the business environment becomes more dynamic, the importance of emotional intelligence in leadership amplifies. Leaders with high emotional intelligence can navigate through uncertainties, manage diverse teams effectively, and develop a resilient organizational culture.

Challenges due to Workplace Stress

In the fast-paced, dynamic landscape of the modern workplace, leaders face a formidable challenge – navigating the delicate balance between productivity and the well-being of their teams. Workplace stress and burnout have emerged as significant issues, prompting a closer look at the role of leadership in developing a healthy work environment and understanding the consequences of leadership styles that contribute to stress.

The Role of Leadership in Developing a Healthy Work Environment:

Leaders play a pivotal role in shaping the work environment. A healthy workplace is not just about meeting targets; it's about creating a space where individuals feel valued, supported, and motivated. Leaders who prioritize employee well-being contribute to a positive workplace culture. They recognize the importance of work-life balance, open communication, and developing a sense of community within the team.

Consequences of Leadership Styles that Contribute to Stress:

Leadership styles significantly influence the stress levels within an organization. Autocratic leadership, characterized by rigid control and limited employee input, can contribute to heightened stress. On the contrary, transformational leadership, which focuses on inspiration, shared vision, and individual development, tends to create a more positive and supportive work environment.

Understanding Workplace Stress:

Workplace stress is a complex interplay of various factors – unrealistic workload, lack of clarity in roles, poor communication, and insufficient support. Leaders need to be attuned to the signs of stress within their teams, such as decreased productivity, increased absenteeism, or changes in behavior. Identifying stressors early allows leaders to address issues proactively.

Preventing Burnout Through Leadership Practices:

Burnout, an advanced stage of chronic workplace stress, is detrimental to both individuals and organizations. Leaders can adopt preventive measures, such as setting realistic expectations, providing resources, and promoting a culture of appreciation. Flexibility in work arrangements and regular check-ins can go a long way in preventing burnout.

Promoting a Culture of Well-being:

Leadership goes beyond task delegation; it involves creating an environment where individuals thrive. Prioritizing employee mental health, offering resources like stress management programs, and encouraging a healthy work-life balance contribute to a culture of well-being. Leaders who champion such initiatives not only reduce stress but also develop loyalty and commitment within their teams.

Challenges due to Communication Breakdown

Effective communication is the backbone of any successful team. However, in the realm of diverse teams, unique challenges can arise, leading to communication breakdowns. Let's explore these challenges and the misalignments that can occur between leaders and team members.

1. Diverse Teams: Diversity in teams brings together individuals with varied experiences, cultures, and communication styles. While this diversity is a strength, it can also present challenges. The tapestry of perspectives, if not woven together effectively, may lead to misunderstandings, misinterpretations, and communication gaps.

Embracing Inclusive Communication Leaders must develop an environment where every team member feels heard and valued. Encouraging open dialogue, active listening, and recognizing the richness of diverse perspectives can bridge the communication gap in diverse teams.

2. Language and Cultural Barriers: In a globalized world, teams often span continents and time zones. Language nuances and cultural differences can pose significant challenges. Messages may be unintentionally distorted, leading to confusion and a breakdown in effective communication.

Cultural Sensitivity Training Leaders should invest in cultural sensitivity training to equip team members with the skills to navigate diverse communication styles. Encouraging a culture of asking clarifying questions and seeking feedback can minimize language and cultural barriers.

3. Hierarchical Misalignments: Communication breakdowns can stem from hierarchical misalignments, where leaders and team members operate on different wavelengths. When team members feel their voices are unheard or opinions undervalued, the communication flow falters.

Flatten the Hierarchy Leaders need to create an inclusive environment where team members feel comfortable expressing their thoughts. Implementing open-door policies, regular check-ins, and team forums can break down hierarchical barriers and promote transparent communication.

4. Technological Overload: In today's digital age, reliance on various communication channels can lead to technological overload. Important messages may get lost in a sea of emails, instant messages, and virtual meetings, resulting in a breakdown of effective communication.

Streamline Communication Channels Leaders should streamline communication channels and emphasize the use of tools that enhance rather than hinder effective communication. Clear guidelines on communication platforms and periodic evaluations can prevent technological overload.

5. Misalignment of Goals: Effective communication thrives on a shared understanding of goals and objectives. When team members and leaders are not aligned on overarching goals, the communication breakdown is inevitable.

Establish Clear Objectives Leaders must ensure that team members understand the broader organizational goals and how their contributions fit into the larger picture. Regularly revisiting and reinforcing these objectives can prevent misalignments.

Mindfulness and Leadership Challenges

At the heart of mindfulness lie fundamental principles that, when adopted, can transform the way we lead. Mindfulness is about cultivating a heightened awareness of the present moment, free from judgment. It involves acknowledging our thoughts and feelings without being overwhelmed by them.

The principles include:

Present Moment Awareness: Mindfulness encourages leaders to be fully present in each moment, appreciating the current reality rather than dwelling on the past or anticipating the future.

Non-Judgmental Acceptance: It involves observing thoughts and emotions without passing judgment. Leaders learn to accept and understand their own and others' experiences without criticism.

Observation of Thoughts: Mindfulness entails observing thoughts as they arise, understanding their transient nature, and not allowing them to dictate actions impulsively.

Focused Attention: Leaders practice directing their attention intentionally, developing concentration and minimizing distractions.

Historical Context and Application in Leadership: To appreciate the application of mindfulness in leadership, let's go deep into its historical roots and draw insights from its practical implementation.

Buddhist Origins: Mindfulness traces its origins to Buddhist meditation practices. In Buddhism, mindfulness, or 'sati,' is a cornerstone of mental cultivation. It involves a conscious awareness of thoughts, feelings, and actions.

Application in Leadership: Mindfulness principles find resonance in leadership by shaping the way leaders engage with themselves, their teams, and the challenges they face.

Self-Aware Leadership: Mindfulness develops self-awareness, enabling leaders to understand their motivations, reactions, and biases. This self-awareness forms the foundation for authentic leadership.

Enhanced Decision-Making: By staying present in decision-making processes, leaders can make more informed choices, considering immediate realities and long-term consequences.

Emotional Regulation: Mindfulness equips leaders with tools to regulate their emotions, responding to situations calmly rather than reacting impulsively. This emotional regulation contributes to a positive work environment.

Cultivating Empathy: The non-judgmental acceptance encouraged by mindfulness enhances leaders' ability to empathize with their team members, developing stronger connections and collaboration.

Understanding mindfulness involves not only grasping its principles but also recognizing its historical evolution and practical relevance in the context of leadership. As we proceed in this exploration, we'll witness how these principles come to life in the daily leadership practices of those who adopt mindfulness.

1. Mindful Decision-Making

Effective leadership hinges on the ability to make sound decisions, and the practice of mindfulness can be a game-changer in this arena. Here, we will explore the profound impact of mindfulness on decision-making processes and go deep into practical strategies for cultivating mindfulness in the decision-making realm.

The Impact of Mindfulness on Decision-Making:

Clarity in Complexity: Mindfulness invites leaders to approach decisions with a clear and focused mind. When faced with complexity, a mindful leader acknowledges the multitude of variables, examines them with a calm perspective, and navigates through the intricacies with clarity. This ensures that decisions are not clouded by impulsive reactions but are grounded in a deep understanding of the situation.

Emotional Intelligence at Play: Decision-making involves a delicate interplay of emotions. Mindfulness cultivates emotional intelligence, enabling leaders to recognize and manage their emotions. This self-awareness allows for decisions that are not swayed by personal biases or reactive emotions. Instead, mindful leaders can respond with empathy and consider the emotional impact of their choices on others.

Resilience in Decision-Making: In the face of challenges or unexpected outcomes, mindful leaders exhibit resilience. They understand that not all decisions will lead to the intended results, but by embracing a mindful approach, they can adapt and learn from the outcomes. This resilience ensures that setbacks are viewed as opportunities for growth rather than insurmountable obstacles.

Strategies for Cultivating Mindfulness in Decision-Making:

Cultivate Present-Moment Awareness: Mindful decision-making starts with being fully present in the moment. Leaders can develop this awareness through practices like meditation, deep breathing, or simply taking a moment of intentional pause before making decisions. This allows for a clear and focused mind.

Practice Non-Judgmental Observation: Encourage leaders to observe their thoughts without judgment. When faced with a decision, instead of immediately labeling thoughts as good or bad, leaders can neutrally observe them. This non-judgmental stance develops a more objective evaluation of options.

Integrate Mindful Listening: Decision-making involves inputs from various stakeholders. Mindful leaders actively listen to different perspectives, valuing each input without immediate judgment. This practice ensures that decisions are informed by a comprehensive understanding of the diverse viewpoints involved.

Implement Reflective Practices: After a decision is made, leaders can engage in reflective practices. This involves revisiting the decision, assessing its impact, and learning from the process. Reflection allows leaders to continuously refine their decision-making skills through mindfulness.

Therefore, mindful decision-making is a cornerstone of effective leadership. By incorporating mindfulness into the decision-making process, leaders can navigate complexities with clarity, leverage emotional intelligence, exhibit resilience, and develop a culture of continuous learning. The strategies outlined provide a roadmap for leaders to infuse mindfulness into their decision-making practices, ensuring that each choice aligns with their values and contributes to organizational success.

Building Emotional Intelligence through Mindfulness

Emotional intelligence, the ability to understand and manage emotions effectively, is a cornerstone of successful leadership. We go deep into the profound connection between mindfulness and the development of emotional intelligence, exploring how it becomes a guiding light in navigating interpersonal relationships.

Understanding Emotional Intelligence: Emotional intelligence involves recognizing and understanding our own emotions and those of others. It encompasses empathy, self-awareness, self-regulation, motivation, and effective interpersonal relationships. Mindfulness serves as a powerful tool to nurture these aspects.

Mindfulness as a Catalyst: At its essence, mindfulness is about being present in the moment without judgment. This mental state provides a fertile ground for developing emotional intelligence. By cultivating mindfulness, leaders can enhance their self-awareness, recognizing and understanding their emotional responses to various situations.

Self-Regulation through Mindfulness: Mindfulness empowers leaders to regulate their emotional responses, preventing impulsive reactions in challenging situations. When faced with stress or adversity, a mindful leader can pause, reflect on their emotions, and respond with a measured and thoughtful approach. This self-regulation is key to effective leadership.

Cultivating Empathy: A mindful leader naturally develops empathy – the ability to understand and share the feelings of others. Mindfulness encourages an open, non-judgmental awareness of others' emotions. By being fully present in conversations and interactions, leaders can tune into the emotional cues of their team, developing a culture of empathy and understanding.

Mindfulness in Interpersonal Relationships: Navigating relationships is a vital aspect of leadership. Mindfulness enables leaders to engage in deep, meaningful connections with their team members. By listening attentively, being fully present, and responding with empathy, leaders can build trust and strengthen the bonds within the team.

Practical Techniques for Leaders: To integrate mindfulness into daily leadership practices, leaders can engage in simple yet impactful techniques. These may include regular mindfulness meditation, mindful breathing exercises, or incorporating moments of reflection into their routines. These practices contribute to the continuous development of emotional intelligence.

Mindfulness for Team Dynamics: Applying mindfulness principles to team dynamics creates a positive ripple effect. Leaders can encourage mindfulness practices within the team, developing a collaborative and emotionally intelligent work environment. This shared mindfulness contributes to enhanced communication, reduced conflict, and improved overall well-being.

Hence, the marriage of mindfulness and emotional intelligence is a transformative journey for leaders. By embracing mindfulness as a tool for self-awareness, self-regulation, and empathy, leaders can navigate interpersonal relationships with grace and authenticity. This serves as a guide for leaders seeking to harness the power of mindfulness to build emotional intelligence and develop positive connections within their teams.

Stress Reduction and Resilience in Mindful Leadership

Leadership, as noble a pursuit as it is, often comes with its fair share of stress and challenges. We will explore the realm of stress reduction and resilience, exploring mindfulness techniques that can serve as powerful tools for leaders navigating the complexities of their roles.

Mindfulness Techniques for Stress Reduction:

Breath Awareness: One of the simplest yet most effective mindfulness techniques is conscious breathing. By directing attention to the breath, leaders can anchor themselves in the present moment, alleviating stress and promoting mental clarity.

Body Scan Meditation: Leaders can practice body scan meditations, systematically focusing on each part of the body to release tension. This technique not only reduces physical stress but also enhances self-awareness.

Mindful Walking: Encouraging leaders to engage in mindful walking – paying full attention to each step – provides a refreshing break during hectic days. It develops a mental reset, reducing the accumulation of stress.

Mindful Listening: Stress often arises from miscommunication. Mindful leaders practice active, non-judgmental listening. By fully engaging in conversations without preconceived notions, they develop understanding and reduce interpersonal stress.

Developing Resilience in the Face of Leadership Challenges:

Acceptance of Impermanence: Mindful leaders understand that challenges are transient. Embracing the impermanence of difficulties enables them to maintain perspective, knowing that every challenge is an opportunity for growth.

Cultivating a Growth Mindset: Resilience thrives in a growth mindset. Mindful leaders perceive setbacks as opportunities to learn and adapt. This mindset develops a positive approach to challenges, promoting resilience in the face of adversity.

Building a Supportive Network: Mindful leaders recognize the importance of a strong support system. Whether through mentorship, peer collaboration, or personal connections, having a network to lean on enhances resilience during challenging times.

Practicing Self-Compassion: Leaders often carry the weight of responsibility. Mindfulness encourages self-compassion, allowing leaders to acknowledge their humanity, forgive themselves for mistakes, and approach challenges with a kind and understanding mindset.

By incorporating these mindfulness techniques into their leadership journey, individuals can not only reduce stress but also develop the resilience needed to weather the storms of leadership challenges. Remember, a mindful leader is not immune to stress but possesses the tools to navigate it with grace, ensuring sustained effectiveness in their leadership role.

Implementation of Mindful Leadership

In the dynamic landscape of leadership, the concept of mindful leadership isn't just a theory; it's a practical approach that unfolds in real-world scenarios. Let's go through some compelling examples of successful mindful leadership to illuminate how this approach translates into action.

1. Sundar Pichai - Google's Mindful Visionary: As the CEO of Google and Alphabet, Sundar Pichai embodies mindful leadership. His approach is rooted in the understanding that innovation flourishes in an environment where employees feel valued and empowered. Pichai develops a workplace culture that encourages creativity, inclusivity, and work-life balance. By prioritizing mindfulness, he ensures that decisions are made with a long-term perspective, promoting both individual well-being and organizational success.

2. Oprah Winfrey - Mindful Empowerment: Oprah Winfrey, the media mogul, is celebrated for her mindful leadership style. Throughout her career, she has championed authenticity, self-awareness, and empowerment. By creating spaces for open dialogue, embracing vulnerability, and practicing active listening, Oprah has built connections that resonate globally. Her commitment to mindfulness has empowered not only her own journey but also inspired countless individuals to adopt their authentic selves.

3. Alan Mulally - Ford's Turnaround Leader: Alan Mulally, the former CEO of Ford, executed one of the most remarkable turnarounds in the automotive industry. His mindful leadership during a crisis involved transparent communication, collaboration, and a focus on the bigger picture. Mulally created a culture where team members felt safe sharing information and ideas, developing a collaborative environment that propelled Ford to success. His approach

showcases how mindfulness can guide leaders through turbulent times with resilience and strategic clarity.

4. Indra Nooyi - Purpose-Driven Leadership: As the former CEO of PepsiCo, Indra Nooyi's mindful leadership centered on purpose and sustainability. She recognized the importance of aligning business goals with societal and environmental well-being. By prioritizing the long-term impact of decisions, Nooyi transformed PepsiCo into a socially responsible and environmentally conscious entity. Her example demonstrates how mindful leadership can drive success while contributing positively to the world.

5. Marc Benioff - Salesforce's Mindful Trailblazer: Marc Benioff, the founder and CEO of Salesforce, is known for blending business success with mindful practices. His commitment to creating a workplace that values equality, philanthropy, and mindfulness sets a powerful example. Benioff's implementation of mindfulness programs at Salesforce underscores his belief

that personal well-being is integral to professional success.

In these examples, we witness mindful leadership in action, where leaders prioritize values, authenticity, and the well-being of individuals and the broader community. The impact of their mindful approaches resonates not only within their organizations but also across industries, emphasizing that mindful leadership is not just a philosophy but a transformative force with tangible, positive outcomes in the real world.

The application of mindfulness has emerged as a transformative force. To understand its real impact, following case studies will illustrate mindful leadership in action, showcasing tangible positive outcomes.

Case Study 1: Google's Mindful Leadership Program

In the tech giant Google, mindful leadership isn't just a philosophy but a structured program. By integrating mindfulness practices into their leadership development,

Google aimed to enhance self-awareness and emotional intelligence among its leaders. The outcome was a more engaged and resilient leadership team, developing a positive work culture.

Case Study 2: Aetna's Mindfulness Initiative

Aetna, a health insurance company, implemented a mindfulness program for its employees. The results were striking – a 28% reduction in stress levels, a 20% improvement in sleep quality, and enhanced overall well-being. This case exemplifies how incorporating mindfulness can contribute not only to leadership effectiveness but also to the well-being of the entire workforce.

Case Study 3: The Impact of Mindful Leadership in Healthcare

In the healthcare sector, where the stakes are high, mindful leadership has demonstrated remarkable outcomes. Studies conducted in healthcare settings reveal that leaders trained in mindfulness exhibit improved decision-making, reduced burnout, and enhanced patient care. These positive shifts highlight the potential of mindfulness in developing resilience and empathy in high-pressure environments.

Case Study 4: Mindful Leadership in Educational Institutions

Educational leaders are also recognizing the benefits of mindfulness. In a study conducted in schools, administrators who underwent mindful leadership training reported a significant reduction in stress levels and an improvement in interpersonal relationships. This ripple effect extended to teachers and students, creating a more positive and conducive learning environment.

Case Study 5: Mindful Leadership in Non-Profit Organizations

Non-profit organizations are embracing mindful leadership to navigate challenges and drive positive change. Case studies in this sector showcase how leaders, by incorporating mindfulness practices, develop collaboration, strategic thinking, and a heightened sense of purpose among team members. This, in turn, amplifies the organization's impact on the communities it serves.

These case studies underscore the versatile application of mindful leadership across diverse sectors. From corporate giants to healthcare, education, and non-profits, the positive outcomes are evident – enhanced well-being, improved decision-making, increased resilience, and a more profound impact on organizational success.

Finally, these real-world examples illuminate the profound impact of mindful leadership in action. By weaving mindfulness into leadership practices, organizations not only empower their leaders but also create environments that nurture the holistic well-being of their teams and, ultimately, the success of the entire enterprise.

Mindful Team Building

Building an effective team is not merely about assembling individuals; it's about forging a collective identity and purpose. Mindful team building is a practice that goes beyond conventional strategies, delving into the realm of developing a culture of mindfulness within teams.

Understanding Mindful Team Building: Mindful team building involves creating an environment where team members are encouraged to be fully present, open, and engaged. It's about cultivating awareness, both of oneself and others, and weaving these individual threads into a cohesive and harmonious tapestry.

The Foundations of Mindful Teams: Imagine a team as a garden, each member a unique flower contributing to the overall beauty. Mindful team building involves nurturing the soil of communication, trust, and collaboration. Much like a gardener tends to every plant's unique needs, a mindful team leader acknowledges and values each team member's strengths and perspectives.

Cultivating Mindfulness within Teams:

Mindful Communication: In a mindful team, communication is more than just conveying information. It's about actively listening, understanding, and responding with intention. By developing mindful communication, teams can reduce misunderstandings and enhance overall effectiveness.

Building Trust: Trust is the foundation of any successful team. Mindful team building emphasizes the importance of trust-building activities, where team members learn to rely on one another, creating a sense of psychological safety and cohesion.

Collaboration with Intent: Mindful teams understand the power of collaboration. They work together with a shared purpose, recognizing that the collective effort often surpasses individual contributions. This shared intent creates a synergy that propels the team towards its goals.

Resilience in Diversity: A mindful team accepts diversity as a strength rather than a challenge. Team building activities encourage understanding and appreciation of each member's unique background, skills, and perspectives. This diversity becomes a source of resilience and adaptability.

Practical Strategies for Mindful Team Building:

Mindful Retreats: Organize mindful retreats where team members engage in activities that promote self-awareness, team cohesion, and relaxation.

Mindful Meetings: Begin team meetings with short mindfulness exercises, developing a focused and present mindset conducive to effective collaboration.

Team-Building Workshops: Conduct workshops focused on building trust, improving communication, and enhancing collective problem-solving skills.

Shared Mindfulness Practices: Encourage team members to adopt mindfulness practices individually, such as meditation or gratitude journaling, promoting a shared commitment to well-being.

Understanding Mindful Team Building

Mindful team building goes beyond conventional approaches. It is centered on creating an environment where team members are encouraged to be present, engaged, and aware of their individual and collective strengths. Mindfulness practices are seamlessly woven into team-building exercises, creating a space for authentic connection and collaboration.

Mindfulness Practices in Team Building:

Mindful Listening Sessions: Begin team-building sessions with mindful listening exercises. Team members gather in a circle, and one person speaks while others practice deep, attentive listening. This not only develops better communication but also creates a sense of being heard and understood.

Collaborative Mindful Breathing: Incorporate mindfulness breathing exercises into collaborative activities. This not only helps in reducing stress but also promotes a sense of unity as the team breathes together. It's a simple yet powerful way to synchronize energies and develop a shared experience.

Mindful Problem Solving: Approach problem-solving activities with a mindful lens. Encourage the team to approach challenges with a calm and focused mindset. Mindfulness helps in reframing problems, promoting creative thinking, and developing resilience in the face of obstacles.

Gratitude Circles: Create moments of reflection and gratitude within the team. Team members take turns expressing gratitude for the contributions of others. This practice cultivates a positive and appreciative team culture, strengthening interpersonal connections.

Mindful Movement Activities: Integrate mindful movement, such as yoga or walking meditations, into team-building sessions. These activities not only enhance physical well-being but also promote a sense of collective purpose and shared experience.

Benefits of Mindful Team Building:

Enhanced Communication: Mindful team building facilitates open and effective communication. When team members are present and attentive, misunderstandings are minimized, and collaboration flourishes.

Strengthened Relationships: Mindfulness practices deepen connections among team members. Shared experiences of mindfulness create a sense of camaraderie and understanding, strengthening interpersonal relationships.

Improved Problem Solving: Teams that practice mindfulness are better equipped to approach problem-solving with clarity and creativity. The collective mindfulness enhances the team's ability to navigate challenges effectively.

Increased Resilience: Mindful team building instills a sense of resilience in the team. By developing a calm and focused mindset, teams can navigate uncertainties and setbacks with greater adaptability.

Positive Team Culture: Mindful team building contributes to the creation of a positive team culture. The infusion of mindfulness promotes a supportive and inclusive environment where team members feel valued and motivated.

Incorporating mindfulness into team-building activities not only enhances the overall team dynamics but also lays the foundation for a resilient, communicative, and high-performing team. As leaders adopt mindful team building, they pave the way for a workplace culture that prioritizes collaboration, well-being, and collective success.

Training Programs for Mindful Leadership

In the dynamic landscape of leadership, the integration of mindfulness can be a game-changer. But how do we introduce and nurture mindful leadership within an organization? Let's deep dive into the world of training programs designed to develop and implement mindful leadership.

Understanding the Need: Before diving into training programs, it's crucial to recognize the need for mindful leadership. The fast-paced, ever-changing business environment demands leaders who can navigate uncertainty, make informed decisions, and develop positive workplace cultures. Mindful leadership, with its focus on self-awareness and holistic understanding, becomes essential in this context.

Key Components of Mindful Leadership Training:

Introduction to Mindfulness:

Provide a foundational understanding of mindfulness principles.

Explore the benefits of mindfulness in personal and professional contexts.

Offer practical techniques for incorporating mindfulness into daily routines.

Self-Reflection and Awareness:

Guide participants in self-reflection exercises to enhance self-awareness.

Explore personal values, strengths, and areas for growth.

Help participants recognize their automatic reactions and habitual patterns.

Emotional Intelligence Development:

Introduce concepts of emotional intelligence and its significance in leadership.

Provide tools for recognizing, understanding, and managing emotions.

Develop empathy and effective communication skills.

Mindful Decision-Making:

Cultivate the ability to make decisions with clarity and focus.

Train leaders to consider the long-term impact of decisions.

Offer techniques for navigating challenging decisions mindfully.

Resilience Building:

Equip leaders with tools to navigate stress and adversity.

Provide strategies for maintaining balance and well-being.

Encourage a resilient mindset in the face of challenges.

Effective Communication Training:

Explore mindful communication techniques.

Emphasize active listening and developing open dialogue.

Provide scenarios and role-playing exercises for practical application.

Implementation Strategies:

Leadership Buy-In:

Ensure that organizational leaders champion the importance of mindful leadership.

Demonstrate the positive impact of mindfulness on leadership effectiveness.

Tailored Programs:

Customize training programs to align with the organization's goals and values.

Consider the unique challenges and dynamics of the industry and workforce.

Continuous Evaluation:

Implement regular assessments to gauge the effectiveness of training programs.

Seek feedback from participants to make necessary adjustments.

Integration into Culture:

Integrate mindful leadership principles into the organizational culture.

Encourage leaders to model mindful behavior and develop a supportive environment.

Training programs for mindful leadership are not just an investment in skill development; they are a commitment to cultivating a workplace culture rooted in awareness, compassion, and effectiveness. As organizations adopt the transformative potential of mindful leadership, these programs serve as the guiding light, equipping leaders with the tools needed to navigate the complexities of leadership with clarity and purpose.

Leadership is not just a position; it's a continuous journey of growth and self-discovery.

Training for Mindful Leadership: Mindfulness is a skill that can be cultivated through training programs. These programs often incorporate meditation, self-awareness exercises, and emotional intelligence workshops. Participants learn to be present, manage stress, and develop a deep understanding of their leadership styles.

Key Components of Training:

Meditation Practices: Mindful leadership training often includes various meditation techniques. These practices help leaders develop focus, emotional regulation, and a heightened awareness of the present moment.

Emotional Intelligence Workshops: Understanding and managing emotions is fundamental to mindful leadership. Workshops on emotional intelligence enable leaders to navigate complex interpersonal dynamics with empathy and self-awareness.

Communication Skills Development: Mindful leaders excel in effective communication. Training programs emphasize transparent and compassionate communication, developing a positive and collaborative organizational culture.

Resilience Building: Leadership is inevitably accompanied by challenges. Mindful leadership training equips leaders with tools to build resilience, enabling them to navigate setbacks with grace and determination.

Assessing Impact on Leadership Effectiveness: Measuring the impact of mindful leadership training is crucial for organizational success. It involves evaluating changes in leadership behavior, team dynamics, and overall workplace culture. Here's how the impact can be assessed:

Behavioral Observations: Trainers and organizational leaders can observe changes in leaders' behavior post-training. Are leaders more present, empathetic, and communicative?

Employee Feedback: Collecting feedback from team members provides valuable insights. Are employees experiencing a positive shift in their leaders' approach? Are communication and collaboration improving?

Performance Metrics: Assessing key performance indicators before and after training can indicate improvements. This might include productivity, employee engagement, and overall team performance.

Organizational Climate Surveys: Surveys focused on workplace climate, conducted periodically, can reveal the broader impact of mindful leadership on the organization. Are employees reporting a healthier work environment?

Case Study: Impact Assessment in XYZ Corporation: In XYZ Corporation, a mindful leadership training program was implemented. Post-training, leaders exhibited enhanced communication, improved team collaboration, and a noticeable reduction in stress levels. Employee surveys reflected increased job satisfaction and a positive shift in the organizational climate.

Training programs for mindful leadership are instrumental in shaping effective leaders. Regular assessment of their impact ensures that organizations are not just investing in training but reaping the benefits of a mindful leadership culture. As we move forward, let's explore how mindful leadership can be integrated into everyday practices and institutionalized for sustained growth.

Overcoming Resistance and Obstacles

Addressing Skepticism

In the world of leadership, mindfulness has emerged as a powerful tool, yet it often encounters skepticism and misconceptions. Let's address some common doubts and obstacles surrounding mindfulness in leadership, unraveling its true potential.

1. Mindfulness is a Trendy Buzzword Some view mindfulness as a passing trend, dismissing it as a buzzword lacking substance. In reality, mindfulness is an ancient practice, deeply rooted in various cultures. Its resurgence in leadership circles is a response to the need for authentic, resilient, and compassionate leaders.

2. Mindfulness is Time-Consuming The misconception that mindfulness requires lengthy meditation sessions discourages busy leaders. However, mindfulness doesn't demand hours of meditation. Even short,

regular practices can yield significant benefits, enhancing focus, clarity, and decision-making.

3. Mindfulness is a Quick Fix Leaders may expect instant results from mindfulness, viewing it as a panacea for all challenges. Mindfulness is a journey, not a quick fix. Consistent practice gradually transforms leadership qualities, developing resilience, empathy, and effective decision-making.

4. Fear of the Unknown Resistance often stems from fear of the unknown. Leaders may be hesitant to explore mindfulness due to unfamiliarity. Addressing this requires demystifying mindfulness, emphasizing its simplicity, and highlighting its potential to enhance leadership capabilities.

5. Balancing Mindfulness with Action Some leaders fear that mindfulness might lead to passive inaction. The truth lies in the synergy of mindfulness and action. Mindful leaders are more equipped to make intentional,

thoughtful decisions and navigate challenges with resilience.

6. Cultural Misalignment In organizations with ingrained cultural norms, introducing mindfulness might face resistance. Open communication, demonstrating tangible benefits, and aligning mindfulness with existing values can help bridge this gap.

7. Mindfulness is Exclusively Personal Leaders may question the applicability of mindfulness in a professional context, viewing it as a solely personal practice. However, mindfulness significantly influences professional attributes like effective communication, empathy, and decision-making.

8. Mindfulness is Religious Some associate mindfulness with specific religious practices, creating apprehension. It's crucial to clarify that mindfulness, in a leadership context, is a secular practice focused on self-awareness and emotional intelligence.

Overcoming Skepticism

A Practical Approach To address skepticism, leaders must demystify mindfulness, offering practical insights into its application. Workshops, success stories, and interactive sessions can showcase its tangible benefits. Encouraging a culture of curiosity and experimentation can gradually dissolve doubts, developing a more mindful and resilient leadership culture. Remember, embracing mindfulness isn't about discarding existing leadership skills; it's about enhancing them with a deeper understanding of oneself and others.

Strategies for overcoming resistance among team members

Leadership journeys are seldom smooth rides. In the pursuit of implementing new ideas or introducing changes, leaders often encounter skepticism, resistance, and various obstacles. Addressing these challenges requires strategic approaches and effective leadership skills. Let's explore strategies for overcoming resistance among team members, drawing insights from successful leaders.

Understanding Skepticism: Skepticism often stems from fear of the unknown, concerns about the impact of change, or doubts about the feasibility of proposed ideas. Leaders need to acknowledge and understand these sentiments to address them effectively.

Transparent Communication: One of the most potent tools in a leader's arsenal is transparent communication. Leaders should openly share the rationale behind proposed changes, addressing concerns and emphasizing the potential benefits. Providing a clear roadmap helps team members visualize the positive outcomes.

Engage and Involve: Involving team members in the decision-making process develops a sense of ownership. Seek their inputs, consider their perspectives, and incorporate their feedback when possible. This inclusive approach diminishes resistance and creates a collaborative atmosphere.

Highlight Success Stories: Sharing success stories related to similar changes can inspire confidence. Leaders can illustrate how others have overcome initial skepticism, emphasizing the positive results achieved. Real-life examples serve as powerful motivators.

Provide Continuous Support: Resistance often diminishes when team members feel supported. Leaders should offer guidance, training, and resources to help the team navigate through the changes. A supportive environment encourages individuals to accept new ideas with greater confidence.

Address Concerns Empathetically: Leaders should listen actively to the concerns and objections raised by team members. Demonstrating empathy and addressing these concerns sincerely builds trust. Sometimes, merely acknowledging apprehensions can go a long way in mitigating resistance.

Celebrate Small Wins: Breaking down the larger goal into smaller milestones allows for the celebration of achievements along the way. Recognizing and celebrating small wins boosts morale and reinforces the positive impact of the changes. It helps in gradually building acceptance.

Provide Training and Resources: Equip team members with the necessary skills and resources to navigate through changes successfully. Training programs and resources tailored to the specific needs of the team enhance their capabilities and reduce resistance born out of uncertainty.

Develop a Culture of Continuous Learning: Encourage a culture where learning is viewed as a continuous process. Highlight the growth opportunities that come with embracing change. This perspective shifts the focus from resistance to the personal and professional development that change can bring.

Lead by Example: Leaders must exemplify the change they advocate. Displaying enthusiasm, resilience, and adaptability sets a powerful example for the team. When team members witness their leader actively embracing change, it encourages them to do the same.

In nutshell, addressing skepticism and overcoming resistance is a vital aspect of effective leadership. By employing transparent communication, involving team members, highlighting success stories, providing continuous support, and developing a culture of learning, leaders can navigate these challenges successfully. It's a journey where strategic leadership and a commitment to positive change can transform skepticism into collaboration and obstacles into stepping stones toward progress.

Incorporating Mindfulness into Organizational Culture

Building a mindful organizational culture is not a mere trend; it's a transformative journey that requires navigating resistance and overcoming obstacles. Let's explore the essential steps for seamlessly integrating mindfulness into the organizational fabric.

Understanding Mindful Organizational Culture: Before beginning the journey, it's crucial to comprehend what a mindful organizational culture entails. This culture is marked by openness, awareness, and a collective commitment to present-moment engagement. It nurtures a workplace where employees can bring their whole selves to work, developing creativity, collaboration, and well-being.

Steps for Integration:

1. Leadership Alignment: The journey begins at the top. Leadership alignment is paramount for successful integration. When leaders embody mindfulness, it sets the tone

for the entire organization. Workshops, training, and coaching can help leaders understand and adopt the principles of mindfulness.

2. Employee Engagement: Mindfulness is most potent when it becomes a shared experience. Engage employees through workshops, seminars, and interactive sessions. These initiatives can introduce them to mindfulness practices, such as meditation and mindful breathing, making it accessible and relatable.

3. Create Mindful Spaces: Design physical spaces that encourage mindfulness. This could range from designated quiet areas for reflection to incorporating natural elements that promote a sense of calm. The physical environment plays a crucial role in reinforcing the cultural shift toward mindfulness.

4. Integration into Policies: Integrate mindfulness into organizational policies. This can include incorporating mindfulness

breaks into the daily schedule, encouraging flexible work hours, and emphasizing the importance of maintaining a healthy work-life balance.

5. Communication and Training: Effective communication is key. Regularly communicate the benefits of mindfulness and how it aligns with the organizational goals. Provide training sessions to equip employees with practical tools for incorporating mindfulness into their daily routines.

Creating a mindful organizational culture is not just a trend; it's a strategic move towards developing a healthier, more productive workplace.

Why Mindfulness Matters in Organizational Culture: A mindful organizational culture prioritizes the well-being of its members, encouraging a positive work environment. This approach recognizes that a healthy, focused, and resilient workforce contributes to the overall success of the organization. By integrating mindfulness practices, organizations aim to enhance employee satisfaction, productivity, and collaboration.

Implementing Mindfulness Practices: Integrating mindfulness into an organizational culture involves a systematic approach. From leadership to frontline staff, everyone plays a crucial role. Leaders can set the tone by practicing mindfulness themselves and encouraging others to do the same. Providing mindfulness training programs and resources, such as meditation sessions or stress-relief workshops, can make these practices accessible to all employees.

Overcoming Resistance and Obstacles: While the benefits of mindfulness are significant, the path to a mindful culture may encounter resistance and obstacles. Here are common challenges and strategies to overcome them:

Perceived Time Constraints: Employees might resist mindfulness practices, citing time constraints. To address this, organizations can integrate brief, impactful mindfulness exercises into daily routines, making them easily achievable.

Cultural Mismatch: In some cases, organizational cultures may clash with mindfulness principles. This challenge requires open communication, emphasizing how mindfulness aligns with organizational values and goals.

Leadership Resistance: If leadership is not fully on board, the implementation may face hurdles. Overcoming this requires educating leaders on the tangible benefits of mindfulness for both individuals and the organization.

Skepticism and Misconceptions: Some individuals may be skeptical about the effectiveness of mindfulness. Offering educational sessions and sharing success stories can help dispel misconceptions.

Lack of Resources: Organizations with limited resources may struggle to implement mindfulness programs. In such cases, focusing on cost-effective strategies and leveraging available resources becomes crucial.

Building a Mindful Organizational Culture: Building a mindful organizational culture is an ongoing process. It involves developing an environment where mindfulness is not just encouraged but becomes an integral part of how work is approached. By consistently addressing challenges, organizations can create a culture that values presence, emotional intelligence, and collective well-being.

Way forward, we will explore how to overcome resistance and obstacles in more detail, providing practical insights and strategies to ensure a successful integration of mindfulness practices into organizational culture.

Conclusion

In our exploration of mindful leadership, we've journeyed through the realms of clarity, focus, emotional intelligence, resilience, effective communication, and empathy. As we conclude, let's reflect on the essence of mindful leadership and how it can shape a brighter future for leaders and their organizations.

The Ripple Effect: Just as a pebble creates ripples in a pond, mindful leadership has a ripple effect on those it touches. A mindful leader's clarity becomes a guiding light for the team, focusing their collective efforts toward a shared vision. The emotional intelligence and empathy they exude create a workplace culture steeped in understanding and support.

Adapting to Change: In a world that constantly evolves, mindful leadership provides a compass for navigating change. Leaders who adopt mindfulness are not resistant to change; instead, they respond with flexibility and resilience. This adaptability is crucial in steering organizations through dynamic landscapes and emerging stronger on the other side.

Inspiring Innovation: Mindful leaders create an environment where innovation flourishes. The space they provide for focused thinking allows team members to explore creative solutions. Effective communication, a hallmark of mindful leadership, ensures that ideas flow freely, developing a culture where every voice is heard.

Cultivating Well-Being: Mindful leadership prioritizes the well-being of individuals. Leaders attuned to the present moment recognize the importance of work-life balance, mental health, and a positive workplace environment. This, in turn, contributes to increased employee satisfaction, engagement, and overall organizational success.

A Lasting Legacy: As we've seen in the life of Mahatma Gandhi, the principles of mindful leadership leave a lasting legacy. The impact of a leader's clarity, resilience, and empathetic guidance extends beyond their tenure. It becomes embedded in the organizational culture, influencing future leaders and developing a cycle of positive leadership.

The Journey Continues: Our exploration of mindful leadership is not a destination but a continual journey. The principles discussed serve as guideposts, encouraging leaders to introspect, adapt, and embody mindfulness in their leadership approach. As we navigate the complexities of the modern world, mindful leadership remains a beacon, illuminating the path toward effective, compassionate, and impactful leadership.

In closing, let us carry the torch of mindful leadership forward, recognizing its potential to transform individuals, teams, and organizations. May it inspire leaders to lead with intention, cultivate a culture of mindfulness, and contribute to a world where leadership is not just about achieving goals but about nurturing the collective well-being and growth of all.

Practical Exercise: Mindful Reflection

Start your day with a few minutes of mindful reflection. Find a quiet space, close your eyes, and focus on your breath. Allow thoughts to come and go without judgment. Reflect on your intentions for the day, acknowledging any stressors or distractions.

Daily Action Plan:

Morning Mindfulness: Begin your day with a short mindfulness practice. This could be meditation, deep breathing, or simply being present as you engage in morning activities.

Intention Setting: Before starting tasks, set clear intentions for what you aim to achieve. This helps create a mindful approach to your actions and develops a sense of purpose.

Single-Tasking: Instead of multitasking, focus on one task at a time. This promotes a mindful and concentrated effort, enhancing the quality of your work.

Mindful Breaks: Incorporate short mindful breaks throughout the day. Take a few minutes to breathe deeply, stretch, or practice gratitude, grounding yourself in the present moment.

Reflective Journaling: At the end of the day, spend a few minutes journaling about your experiences. Reflect on moments of mindfulness, challenges faced, and insights gained.

Digital Detox: Allocate specific times for checking emails and messages. Limiting digital distractions develops a more mindful and focused work environment.

Compassion Practice: Practice compassion towards yourself and others. Be aware of your reactions and responses, cultivating empathy in your interactions.

Mindful Communication: Pay attention to your words and how you express yourself. Practice active listening and respond thoughtfully in conversations.

Evening Wind-Down: Wind down with a mindful activity before bedtime. This could be reading, gentle stretching, or another calming practice to promote relaxation.

Gratitude Ritual: End your day by reflecting on three things you're grateful for. This positive focus enhances mindfulness and encourages a sense of fulfillment.

Mindfulness is a journey, not a destination. Adopt these daily actions gradually, allowing them to become integral parts of your leadership approach.

Self-Assessment

Welcome to the Self-Assessment on "The Art of Mindful Leadership." Mindful leadership involves the ability to lead with presence, awareness, and a deep understanding of oneself and others. This self-assessment aims to help you reflect on your current level of mindfulness in leadership roles. As you answer the questions, consider your experiences, attitudes, and behaviors in various leadership situations.

Guidelines:

Honest Reflection: Be sincere in your responses. This assessment is a tool for personal reflection and growth. There are no right or wrong answers, only insights into your current mindful leadership practices.

Consider Leadership Contexts: Reflect on various leadership contexts, including team interactions, decision-making processes, and handling challenging situations. The questions are designed to capture different facets of mindful leadership.

Numerical Scale: Assign a score from 1 to 5 for each question, where:

1: Rarely or Never

2: Occasionally

3: Sometimes

4: Often

5: Always or Consistently

Personal Insights: Use the space provided after each question to jot down any specific insights, realizations, or examples that come to mind. This will help you delve deeper into your mindful leadership journey.

Complete Open-Mindedly: Approach this self-assessment with an open mind. The goal is self-awareness and potential areas for growth. Adopt the opportunity to gain insights into your mindful leadership practices.

Now, let's begin the self-assessment with the understanding that mindful leadership is an ongoing journey of self-discovery and improvement. Take your time, and enjoy the process of reflecting on your mindful leadership skills.

Self-Assessment on The Art of Mindful Leadership

Please use the provided numerical scale (1 to 5) to indicate the extent to which each statement aligns with your mindful leadership practices.

1. Leading with Presence:

I am fully present and engaged during team meetings and discussions.

Insights/Examples:

2. Compassionate Decision-Making:

I consider the impact of decisions on individuals and the team as a whole.

Insights/Examples:

3. Emotional Regulation:

I effectively manage my emotions in challenging situations.

Insights/Examples:

4. Active Listening:

I attentively listen to team members without interrupting or pre-judging.

Insights/Examples:

5. Empowering Team Members:

I encourage and support team members to take initiative and contribute ideas.

Insights/Examples:

6. Adapting to Change:

I navigate and lead others through changes with flexibility and resilience.

Insights/Examples:

7. Maintaining a Learning Mindset:

I see challenges as opportunities for learning and growth.

Insights/Examples:

8. Developing Inclusivity:

I promote an inclusive and diverse environment within the team.

Insights/Examples:

9. Mindful Communication:

I communicate clearly and mindfully, considering the impact of my words.

Insights/Examples:

10. Balancing Work and Well-Being:

I prioritize the well-being of myself and my team amidst work demands.

Insights/Examples:

11. Integrating Mindfulness Practices:

I incorporate mindfulness practices into my daily routine for personal well-being.

Insights/Examples:

12. Recognizing and Managing Stress:

I am aware of stress triggers and employ effective strategies to manage stress.

Insights/Examples:

13. Building Trust:

I actively work on building and maintaining trust within the team.

Insights/Examples:

14. Resolving Conflicts Mindfully:

I approach conflicts with a mindful and constructive mindset.

Insights/Examples:

15. Encouraging Open Communication:

I create an environment where team members feel comfortable sharing ideas and concerns openly.

Insights/Examples:

16. Nurturing Creativity:

I develop a culture that encourages creative thinking and innovation.

Insights/Examples:

17. Being Present in Meetings:

I actively engage and contribute meaningfully during team meetings.

Insights/Examples:

18. Aligning Actions with Values:

My leadership actions consistently reflect the values I promote.

Insights/Examples:

19. Demonstrating Patience:

I remain patient and composed during challenging situations.

Insights/Examples:

20. Encouraging Continuous Improvement:

I advocate for and support ongoing professional development for myself and the team.

Insights/Examples:

21. Building Team Cohesion:

I actively work to create a sense of unity and collaboration among team members.

Insights/Examples:

22. Setting Clear Expectations:

I communicate expectations clearly to avoid misunderstandings within the team.

Insights/Examples:

23. Practicing Gratitude:

I express gratitude and appreciation for the efforts of team members.

Insights/Examples:

24. Instilling a Sense of Purpose:

I inspire the team by developing a shared sense of purpose.

Insights/Examples:

25. Seeking Feedback:

I actively seek feedback from team members to enhance leadership effectiveness.

Insights/Examples:

26. Balancing Empathy and Objectivity:

I strike a balance between empathy and objectivity in decision-making.

Insights/Examples:

27. Encouraging Personal Development:

I support the personal and professional development of team members.

Insights/Examples:

28. Practicing Mindful Delegation:

I delegate tasks mindfully, considering individual strengths and growth opportunities.

Insights/Examples:

29. Adapting Leadership Style:

I adapt my leadership style based on the needs and preferences of the team.

Insights/Examples:

30. Leading by Example:

I consistently model the behaviors and values I expect from the team.

Insights/Examples:

Use this self-assessment as a guide for continuous improvement, developing a mindful leadership approach that positively influences your team and contributes to your personal growth.

Join My Community